T0364116

THE

COFFEE
BEAN

THE

COFFEE BEAN

A Simple Lesson to Create Positive Change

JON GORDON   DAMON WEST

Published by John Wiley & Sons, Inc., Hoboken, New Jersey.
Published simultaneously in Canada.

Illustrations by Rachel Yedam Kim.

For general information on our other products and services or for technical support, please contact our Customer Care Department within the United States at (800) 762-2974, outside the United States at (317) 572-3993 or fax (317) 572-4002.

Wiley publishes in a variety of print and electronic formats and by print-on-demand. Some material included with standard print versions of this book may not be included in e-books or in print-on-demand. If this book refers to media such as a CD or DVD that is not included in the version you purchased, you may download this material at http://booksupport.wiley.com. For more information about Wiley products, visit www.wiley.com.

ISBN 9781119430278 (Hardcover)
ISBN 9781119430865 (ePDF)
ISBN 9781119430988 (ePub)

Printed in the United States of America
SKY10023254_121520

*Jon dedicates this book to Kathryn for overcoming
her circumstances and transforming her world
like a Coffee Bean.*

* * *

*This book is dedicated to my wife, Kendell, and her daughter, Clara.
My favorite Coffee Beans. Love, Damon*

Introduction

In the summer of 2018, Jon Gordon sat in Dabo Swinney's office, just as he had done every training camp since 2012, discussing books they had read and sharing ideas on building great cultures and winning teams. On this occasion, Dabo shared with Jon that he just had a guy speak to his team who had delivered one of the most impactful messages he had ever heard.

That guy was Damon West—and his talk was about the coffee bean. Dabo loved the coffee bean lesson so much that he was even carrying around a little wooden coffee bean key chain that Damon had given him. Jon was intrigued and wanted to know more about Damon and the Coffee Bean message, so he called Damon and asked him to share his story.

Damon's rise, fall, and audacious comeback was one of the most amazing stories Jon had ever heard.

Damon told Jon about the power of the Coffee Bean message and how it transformed his life and led to his improbable and miraculous comeback. Jon knew that the Coffee Bean message needed to be shared with the world and he asked Damon to write this book with him.

Damon and Jon believe the Coffee Bean message is one of the most important and impactful messages on the planet and truly hope this simple story and powerful lesson encourages and inspires you and your team to create positive change.

THE

COFFEE
BEAN

Are you a carrot, an egg, or a coffee bean?

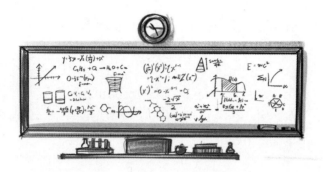

Abraham usually loved science class, but not today. Today, he hated science, school, and everything in his life. As his favorite teacher, Mr. Jackson, scanned the classroom, he noticed Abraham was not his usual self. After class, he told him to stay behind and asked him what was wrong.

Abraham, whom everyone called Abe, told Mr. Jackson how stressed he was about school. He had tests coming up and a big paper due. Not to mention that he was really nervous about the big football game Friday night.

He dreamed of playing football in college and had heard that college scouts were going to be at the game. A win would also bring his team one step closer to a state championship. To make matters worse, his parents were fighting a lot, and had even used the word "divorce" for the first time.

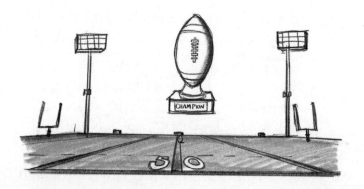

Abe said he tries to ignore all his problems and spends a lot of time on social media and watching videos, but that doesn't help and actually makes him feel more negative and depressed. "It's hard living up to the expectations everyone has when you are playing well, and it's even harder to hear all the negative comments when you're playing badly," he added.

Mr. Jackson nodded, told Abe he knew exactly how he felt, and went to the whiteboard and erased the scientific formula. Then he drew a picture of a carrot inside a pot of water.

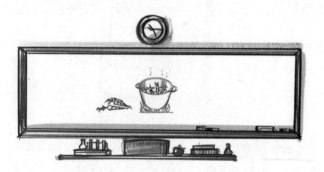

"What happens when you put a carrot in really hot water?" Mr. Jackson asked.

"It gets hot," answered Abe.

"Well, it does more than just get hot," answered Mr. Jackson. "I want you to go home tonight and try it and see what happens."

Abe said he would do it, although he wondered how putting carrots in hot water was going to help him with his problems.

"Oh, and if you've never cooked before, ask for help. I don't want you to burn yourself," Mr. Jackson said with a big smile, as Abe walked out of the classroom.

The next day after class, Abe told Mr. Jackson that the carrot he put into hot water softened after about ten minutes.

"Yes, the carrot was softened and weakened by its environment. It was impacted by the conditions it was in," said Mr. Jackson.

"Sort of like me," Abe said.

"Actually, just like you," Mr. Jackson responded, before going to the board and drawing a picture of an egg inside a pot of water.

"Now, tell me what happens when you put an egg inside a pot of boiling water."

"Oh, this is an easy one," Abe said. "You get hard-boiled eggs. Even I know that."

"Great," Mr. Jackson responded. "The hot water causes the egg to harden. The egg is hardened by its environment and the conditions it's in."

"Unfortunately, it happens to a lot of people as well. They become mean, angry, negative, and sometimes numb because of the difficult environments they are in. They grow to hate life and hate people. Their heart hardens and they lose the desire to love and be loved. I don't want this to happen to you, which is why I'm teaching you this lesson."

"I understand," said Abe, who was beginning to see why Mr. Jackson was talking about carrots and eggs.

"The carrot is weakened and the egg is hardened when put in hot water. I get it," Abe said. "I don't want to be like a carrot or an egg."

"No, you don't," said Mr. Jackson. "But there's one more part of the lesson and experiment you need to experience and understand."

Mr. Jackson erased the picture of the pot with the egg and drew a new picture with a coffee bean inside a pot of water.

"What happens when you put a coffee bean in really hot water?" Mr. Jackson asked.

"I have no idea," answered Abe.

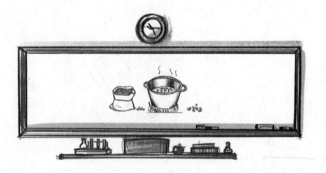

"Well, that's what you need to do next,"
Mr. Jackson said, as he grabbed a few coffee
beans from a jar on his desk and placed them
in Abe's hand. "Go home and put these in
hot water for about an hour and tell me
tomorrow what
happens."

"And be careful you don't burn yourself!"
Mr. Jackson shouted, as Abe left the room.

The next day after class, Abe approached Mr. Jackson and excitedly shared that the coffee beans he put into hot water eventually turned the water into coffee.

"I knew ground coffee beans make coffee," he said, "but I didn't know a coffee bean would do the same."

"Yes, it works the same," Mr. Jackson said, "but it just takes longer."

"It's like magic," Abe said.

"It is," Mr. Jackson answered. "But I prefer to call it transformation."

He then went to the board and drew a picture of three pots side by side with a carrot, an egg, and a coffee bean inside.

"It's one of the simplest and most powerful lessons you will ever learn," Mr. Jackson said as he pointed to the board.

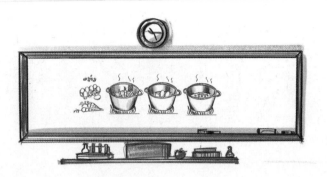

"Life is often like a pot of very hot water. It can be a harsh, stressful, and difficult place. You will find yourself in environments and facing conditions that test who you truly are, and can change, weaken, or harden you if you let them."

"Like all the stuff I'm going through now," Abe said.

"Exactly," Mr. Jackson responded.

"You are feeling the pressure of school, papers, and tests. You are feeling the heat that comes with the expectations of being a great football player. You feel like your parents' marriage is about to boil over. The hate on social media and the negativity in the world is rising; it's all one big pot of boiling water.

"But you have a choice.

"You can be like the carrot that is weakened and softened by its environment.

"You can be like the egg that is hardened by its environment.

"Or, you can be like the coffee bean that transforms its environment.

"And when I look at you, I don't see a carrot. I don't see an egg.

"I see a coffee bean who will overcome challenges and change the world.

"I want you to remember this lesson for the rest of your life. Wherever you go and whatever you do, remember you are a coffee bean and you have the power to transform any environment you are in.

"No matter how hard things get, or how hopeless things look, don't give up. Realize that we don't create our world from the outside in. We create and transform it from the inside out.

"If you think you are a carrot, you will believe the power and forces outside you are more powerful than who you are on the inside, and you will become weaker.

"If you think you are an egg, you will believe the negativity in the world has the power to harden your heart and cause you to become negative like the world.

"But if you know you are a coffee bean, you will not allow the outside world to impact you. You will know that the power inside you is greater than the forces outside you, and with this insight, you will transform your environment and world from the inside out.

"The power is on the inside.
Be the coffee bean."

Mr. Jackson then reached into his pocket, pulled out a coffee bean, and handed it to Abe. "Keep this in your pocket as a reminder of who you are and the power you possess. I know the best is yet to come for you."

Abe left the classroom energized and excited to be a coffee bean and ready to take on the challenges in his life, starting with the big football game Friday night. He was no longer stressed about his paper, school, or his parents' marriage. His perspective had changed, his energy had shifted, and his state of mind was elevated.

That week, when his coach talked during practice about controlling what you can control and not worrying about what the media says or the outcome of the game, Abe knew it simply meant to be a coffee bean.

He told his coach and team the story about the carrot, the egg, and the coffee bean, and he gave coffee beans to his entire team. He told them that it didn't matter where they played or who they were playing. And it didn't matter whether the crowd cheered or booed. The power was not in the stands. The power was inside them.

They played the best game of their lives that Friday night and went on to win the state championship.

Abe, however, was injured in the championship game. In the fourth quarter, with only a few minutes remaining, he made an incredible play to help seal the win but then fell awkwardly to the ground. He couldn't walk and had to hop off the field and watch the final minutes from the sideline.

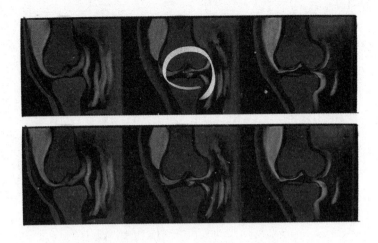

An MRI a few days later revealed that he would need surgery to repair the ACL in his knee. He wondered if it would affect his ability to play in college but didn't let the injury get him down. In the past, a setback like that would have threatened to ruin his life, but instead he thought of ways to turn this negative into a positive.

He decided to start a coffee bean club that was focused on making his school, community, and world a more positive place. So, in addition to going to class and rehabbing his knee, he spent his free time recruiting fellow students to join him in visiting the local elementary schools and reading children's books to the students.

Abe and the club also wrote positive notes to students who seemed to be having a tough time, and they engaged in random acts of kindness. They also made it their mission to post positive messages on social media, and when they did, they used #coffeebean at the end of each post.

Abe told his classmates, "We don't have to allow the negativity on social media to influence us. Instead, we can positively influence social media, one person at a time."

Over the course of the rest of the school year, Abe's knee got stronger and his impact grew. By the end of the school year, it was clear to all that the club had transformed the culture of the school. It was no longer cool to be negative. Instead, it became cool to be a coffee bean and help others.

After high school graduation, Abe went
to the United States Service Academy to
study, serve his country, and play football.
While most college teams didn't recruit
him because of his injury, the U.S. Service
Academy loved his attitude and believed he
had what it took to succeed there.

Within the first few months, Abe realized why attitude was so important at the Academy as he faced the toughest environment and conditions he had ever experienced.

The Academy created a curriculum and a schedule designed to cause the cadets to fail. The cadets couldn't humanly do all that they had to do, so they would fail at something. The Academy found that through failure, most cadets would become stronger, wiser, and better. Those who didn't grow from failure were the ones who quit, and, through this process, they either weeded people out or made them stronger.

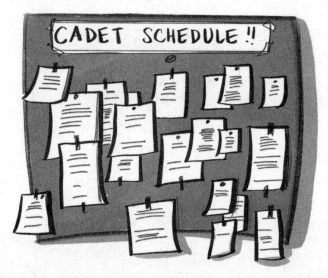

Abe was determined not to be one of the people who quit, and his secret weapon was being a coffee bean.

In the Academy, the water was hotter than ever, but he just saw it as a greater opportunity to transform his environment and not become weakened or hardened by it.

He told himself that failure is not a definition. It's just an event. Just because you fail doesn't mean you are a failure. It's just a situation to overcome and transform. And it will make you stronger if you are willing to learn and grow from it.

He felt the same way about his parents' marriage, which unfortunately ended in divorce. Sure, he was sad it ended, but he wasn't going to let it define his life or his relationship with them. He wanted them to change, but he couldn't make them change. All he could do was love them and help them work it out amicably.

Abe grew as a leader and became a star football player at the Academy. He shared the coffee bean lesson with many of his fellow cadets and teammates, and even his officers, coaches, and teachers.

The football team became one of the most improved teams in the country, and after a few years, the Academy noticed fewer people were quitting. They discovered that, in the past, the cadets weren't quitting because they couldn't handle adversity. They were quitting because they saw themselves as carrots.

Once Abe opened their eyes and helped them realize they could be coffee beans, they stayed the course. The Academy still put the same pressure on everyone and the conditions were just as harsh, but what changed was that the cadets saw the truth about who they were. They began to understand they were no longer victims of their environment. They recognized the power they possessed to overcome and transform their situation.

After graduating from the Academy, Abe went on to serve as a leader in the military and brought his coffee beans with him. Wherever he went and whatever platoon he led, he shared the coffee bean lesson with his soldiers and handed out coffee beans as reminders. They learned from him, but he also learned from them.

In some of the most dangerous places and situations, he saw his soldiers risk their lives for their country and each other.

He learned that love is greater than fear, and that their love and willingness to sacrifice for each other was greater than the fear of a harmful outcome. He had heard that love casts out fear, and now he saw this with his own eyes.

Abe believed that understanding the
interaction of love and fear could fit
perfectly with the lesson of the coffee
bean. So he taught his soldiers that while
fear and worry can weaken or harden you,
love transforms you and the people and
situations around you.

If you know you are a coffee bean who leads and lives with love, fear will have no power over you.

Not surprisingly, Abe's units became some of the most connected, committed, and best-performing units in the military.

When his five years of service were completed, he went back to his home town.

After Abe returned home, he married his high school sweetheart and volunteered as a coach for his old high school team. He loved coaching but had a greater desire to work in business. He and his wife talked a lot about starting a family, and Abe began looking for a job that would support them.

He eventually found a job in sales, and shortly after that his wife became pregnant with their first child. Over the next few years, they had three children.

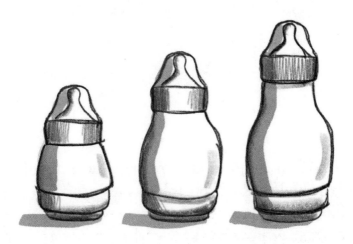

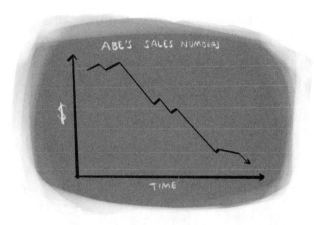

While his family was growing, Abe worked extremely hard at his job to support his family. The problem, however, was that no matter how hard he worked, his sales numbers continued to decline. He suddenly felt a lot of pressure to provide for them, and to make matters worse, his company wasn't doing well because of all the changes in technology and economic forces beyond its control.

Day after day, week after week, as Abe and his company fell short of their sales goals and revenue targets, he became more and more fearful and stressed about their situation and worried about his family's future.

When his wife tried to talk to him about his struggles, he would just say, "I'll figure it out," and walk out of the room. The more his wife tried to support him, the more he shut down.

He stopped seeing his wife and children as gifts, and saw them as obligations he had to support. He looked at the mortgage, the two cars, the doctor bills, and credit card debts, and saw people whose lives depended on him.

One cold winter day, on a Saturday morning, Abe sat in his kitchen alone, drinking a cup of coffee and thinking about his next steps. His wife had taken the kids out of the house to avoid his misery.

Find a new job. Go back into the military. Leave and never come back. These were ideas that came to mind. He placed his coffee cup down and put his face in his hands. He then looked into the cup and could feel the heat rising from the coffee. It was a cold day and yet the coffee was warming him up.

He shook his head. How easy to forget. He had forgotten the lesson that had changed his life years before. He had allowed his environment to weaken and harden him at the same time. He realized how quickly it can happen when adversity hits, your foundation is shaken, and fear sets in.

He went to the store and bought some coffee beans. He put them in a jar on his desk and put one in his pocket. He vowed he wouldn't forget again and would no longer allow his circumstances to define him or his family's future.

When his wife and children returned home, he apologized to them and said, "Today begins day one of being a coffee bean again."

He showed up at work on Monday with resolve, commitment, and belief that he was going to find a way to succeed. And he did.

It didn't take long for his colleagues and leaders to notice his attitude, energy, and results.

While everyone walked around feeling sorry for themselves and longing for the good ol' days, Abe put his head down, worked hard, developed new relationships and opportunities, and created a lot of good days. Within a short time, he was promoted to district sales manager, and a year later, he became a regional sales manager.

Most of the sales people and regional managers complained about their situation and the economy, but Abe taught his team the coffee bean lesson. Together, they focused on what they could control and worked hard with optimism to become the number one region in the company every quarter.

The leaders in the company couldn't help but notice that Abe and his team were doing something different.

With overall sales numbers falling and profits dwindling, they knew they needed to do something to save their company and future. So they promoted Abe to the head of sales and marketing, hoping he could turn things around.

Abe told everyone that instead of being fearful of the future, they were going to love the challenge in front of them.

Night after night, he came home and discussed the problems his company was facing with his wife and children and he got them involved in coming up with solutions.

He wanted his children to learn to become problem solvers and solution seekers instead of blamers and complainers.

He and his wife had decided that they didn't want to teach their children to merely survive. They wanted to teach them how to thrive.

Of course, they discussed the coffee bean often with them, and the kids even got involved in crafting his presentation to the entire company.

At the national sales meeting, Abe presented his plan to win in their minds, win in the offices, win back customers, win in the marketplace, and win the future. The coffee bean lesson was a big part of his presentation, and he shared experiences from his own life's journey to reinforce the message.

For the first time in a long time, people were energized and excited about coming to work and creating the future together.

But for all the optimism and excitement, it wasn't easy and results didn't come overnight. People were still fearful and questioned whether Abe's plan could or would really work. The situation certainly didn't look good.

But Abe didn't waiver. He knew it was just another situation that needed to be transformed, and he kept sharing his plan, his belief, and his coffee bean message with everyone.

And then it happened.

After the company experienced the worst financial quarter in its history, things turned around.

With Abe's help and direction, the company adapted, innovated, added new products and services, eliminated what was no longer working, streamlined operations, and transformed the company with new technology, ideas, and good old-fashioned hard work and grit.

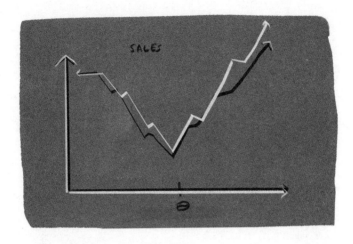

In an industry where most of their competitors were dying, Abe's company was now thriving.

They all saw firsthand the power of the coffee bean.

Abe and his company didn't let the industry and economic conditions change them for the worse. Instead, they changed the industry and the economy for the better.

Experts came from all over the world to study the success and transformation of Abe's company, and he was invited to speak at many conferences.

He felt most energized when talking about the coffee bean, and after a few years he decided it was time to share the coffee bean message with the world.

With his children now in high school and thinking about college, Abe left the comfort of his job to share the coffee bean message with any group, organization, or company that would listen.

He often reflected on his meeting with Mr. Jackson and knew that the coffee bean had changed his life forever. It was his purpose and responsibility to impact the lives of as many people as possible.

And that's
what he did.

For the rest of his life, Abe shared the message of the coffee bean.

He shared it with businesses, schools, sports teams, nonprofits, hospitals, and even children.

He shared it on the biggest stages and in the smallest rooms, and never grew tired of doing it.

The stories of transformation and changed lives kept pouring in, and each note energized him and kept him going, year after year, decade after decade.

As he became an elderly man, people often asked him when he was going to retire but he always responded with a hearty laugh. "I'll stop doing this when coffee beans no longer exist or when I die, whichever comes first."

It wasn't a job or a career, but a life mission, and he knew in the end it didn't matter how much money he had in his bank account or how many awards he received. What mattered most was the difference he had made in people's lives.

THE MISSION

Toward the end of his life, he no longer traveled on airplanes or stood on stages, but he didn't let his aging body keep him from making an impact. After his wife had passed on and his grandchildren were grown, all he had was time and wisdom and he spent his later years giving both away.

He often sat on a bench in a local park near his home, sharing the coffee bean lesson with anyone who would listen.

One day, a high school student who was playing basketball took a break and sat down next to him on the bench. He looked fearful and stressed out, and Abe asked him what was wrong.

The young man proceeded to share how everything in his life was going wrong. He was failing in school, his girlfriend had broken up with him, and he had a big concert coming up with his band that he was really nervous about. Not to mention all the negativity in the world that was bringing him down.

"What's the point of life?" the young man asked.

Abe reached into his pocket and handed the young man a coffee bean and said, "Let me tell you a story about the carrot, the egg, and the coffee bean. . . ."

THE END

About the Authors

JON GORDON has inspired millions of readers around the world. He is the author of 18 books, including six bestsellers: *The Energy Bus, The Carpenter, Training Camp, You Win in the Locker Room First, The Power of Positive Leadership,* and *The Power of a Positive Team.* He is passionate about developing positive leaders, organizations, and teams.

DAMON WEST is a motivational speaker and author of *The Change Agent: How a Former College QB Sentenced to Life in Prison Transformed His World.* Over the past few years, he has been sharing the coffee bean lesson with college football teams such as Clemson, Alabama, Georgia, and Texas, and countless schools and businesses. Damon is passionate about the Coffee Bean message, and loves sharing how it changed his life and how it can change yours, too.

About the Illustrator

RACHEL YEDAM KIM was born and raised in a small town in Korea but moved across the world to study Media Arts at the University of Southern California. She has been drawing and painting for as long as she can remember and has a passion for telling inspiring stories.

When she isn't drawing, you can find her taking street photography, editing wedding videos, and drinking a little too much coffee.

For more illustrations and drawings, visit www.yedamkim.com.

Other Books by Jon Gordon

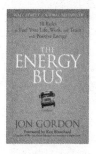

The Energy Bus

A man whose life and career are in shambles learns from a unique bus driver and set of passengers how to overcome adversity. Enjoy an enlightening ride of positive energy that is improving the way leaders lead, employees work, and teams function.

www.TheEnergyBus.com

The No Complaining Rule

Follow a VP of Human Resources who must save herself and her company from ruin, and discover proven principles and an actionable plan to win the battle against individual and organizational negativity.

www.NoComplainingRule.com

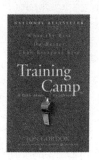

Training Camp

This inspirational story about a small guy with a big heart, and a special coach who guides him on a quest for excellence, reveals the eleven winning habits that separate the best individuals and teams from the rest.

www.TrainingCamp11.com

The Shark and the Goldfish

Delightfully illustrated, this quick read is packed with tips and strategies on how to respond to challenges beyond your control in order to thrive during waves of change.

www.SharkandGoldfish.com

Soup

The newly appointed CEO of a popular soup company is brought in to reinvigorate the brand and bring success back to a company that has fallen on hard times. Through her journey, discover the key ingredients to unite, engage, and inspire teams to create a culture of greatness.

www.Soup11.com

The Seed

Go on a quest for the meaning and passion behind work with Josh, an up-and-comer at his company who is disenchanted with his job. Through Josh's cross-country journey, you'll find surprising new sources of wisdom and inspiration in your own business and life.

www.Seed11.com

One Word

One Word is a simple concept that delivers powerful life change! This quick read will inspire you to simplify your life and work by focusing on just one word for this year. *One Word* creates clarity, power, passion, and life-change. When you find your word, live it, and share it, your life will become more rewarding and exciting than ever.

www.getoneword.com

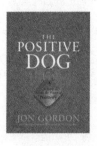

The Positive Dog

We all have two dogs inside of us. One dog is positive, happy, optimistic, and hopeful. The other dog is negative, mad, pessimistic, and fearful. These two dogs often fight inside us, but guess who wins? The one you feed the most. *The Positive Dog* is an inspiring story that not only reveals the strategies and benefits of being positive, but also an essential truth: being positive doesn't just make you better; it makes everyone around you better.

www.feedthepositivedog.com

The Energy Bus for Kids

The illustrated children's adaptation of the bestselling book, *The Energy Bus*, tells the story of George, who, with the help of his school bus driver, Joy, learns that if he believes in himself, he'll find the strength to overcome any challenge. His journey teaches kids how to overcome negativity, bullies, and everyday challenges to be their best.

www.EnergyBusKids.com

The Carpenter

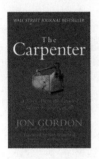

The Carpenter is Jon Gordon's most inspiring book yet—filled with powerful lessons and success strategies. Michael wakes up in the hospital with a bandage on his head and fear in his heart after collapsing during a morning jog. When Michael finds out the man who saved his life is a carpenter, he visits him and quickly learns that he is more than just a carpenter; he is also a builder of lives, careers, people, and teams. In this journey, you will learn timeless principles to help you stand out, excel, and make an impact on people and the world.

www.carpenter11.com

The Hard Hat

A true story about Cornell lacrosse player George Boiardi, *The Hard Hat* is an unforgettable book about a selfless, loyal, joyful, hard-working, competitive, and compassionate leader and teammate, the impact he had on his team and program, and the lessons we can learn from him.

This inspirational story will teach you how to build a great team and be the best teammate you can be.

www.hardhat21.com

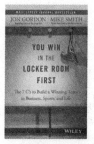

You Win in the Locker Room First

Based on the extraordinary experiences of NFL Coach Mike Smith and leadership expert Jon Gordon, *You Win in the Locker Room First* offers a rare, behind-the-scenes look at one of the most pressure-packed leadership jobs on the planet, and what leaders can learn from these experiences in order to build their own winning teams.

www.wininthelockerroom.com

Thank You and Good Night

Thank You and Good Night is a beautifully illustrated book that shares the heart of gratitude. Jon Gordon takes a little boy and girl on a fun-filled journey from one perfect moonlit night to the next. During their adventurous days and nights, the children explore the people, places, and things they are thankful for.

Life Word

Life Word reveals a simple, powerful tool to help you identify the word that will inspire you to live your best life while leaving your greatest legacy. In the process, you'll discover your *why*, which will help show you how to live with a renewed sense of power, purpose, and passion.

www.getoneword.com/lifeword

The Power of Positive Leadership

The Power of Positive Leadership is your personal coach for becoming the leader your people deserve. Jon Gordon gathers insights from his bestselling fables to bring you the definitive guide to positive leadership. Difficult times call for leaders who are up for the challenge. Results are the byproduct of your culture, teamwork, vision, talent, innovation, execution, and commitment. This book shows you how to bring it all together to become a powerfully positive leader.

www.powerofpositiveleadership.com

The Energy Bus Field Guide

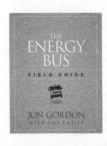

The Energy Bus Field Guide is your roadmap to fueling your life, work, and team with positive energy. The international bestseller, *The Energy Bus*, has helped millions of people from around the world shift to a more positive outlook. This guide is a practical companion to help you *live and share* the ten principles from *The Energy Bus* every day, with real, actionable steps you can immediately put into practice in your life, work, team, and organization.

The Power of a Positive Team

In *The Power of a Positive Team*, Jon Gordon draws upon his unique team building experience, as well as conversations with some of the greatest teams in history, to provide an essential framework of proven practices to empower teams to work together more effectively and achieve superior results.

www.PowerOfAPositiveTeam.com

The Hard Hat for Kids

The Hard Hat for Kids is an illustrated guide to teamwork. Adapted from the bestseller *The Hard Hat*, this uplifting story presents practical insights and life-changing lessons that are immediately applicable to everyday situations, giving kids—and adults—a new outlook on cooperation, friendship, and the selfless nature of true teamwork.

www.HardHatforKids.com

Other Books by Damon West

The Change Agent

The Change Agent tells the true story of a well-raised kid, three-year starting quarterback, and a young person filled with potential . . . until a shocking addiction took hold. Armed with a program of recovery, a renewed faith, and a miraculous second chance at life, Damon emerged from over seven years of prison a changed man. His story of redemption continues to inspire audiences today.